THE BUSINESS SUCCESS GUIDE TO BISON RANCHING

Expert Strategies For Profitable Operations, Market Expansion, Sustainable Practices, And Effective Management In The Industry

RICHMOND HAMILL

© 2024 [RICHMOND HAMILL]. All rights reserved.

Except for brief quotations included in critical reviews and certain other noncommercial uses allowed by copyright law, no part of this book may be reproduced, distributed, or transmitted in any form or by any means, including photocopying, recording, or other electronic or mechanical methods, without the publisher's prior written permission.

Disclaimer

The information presented in this book is based on the author's personal knowledge and understanding of livestock management. The author is not affiliated with any association, company, business, or individual in the livestock industry. All content is provided for informational purposes only and should not be considered as professional advice. Readers are encouraged to seek professional guidance and conduct their own research before making any decisions based on the information contained in this book. The author and publisher disclaim any liability for any adverse effects or consequences resulting from the use of the information contained herein.

TABLE OF CONTENTS

CHAPTER ONE 17

Introduction To Bison Ranching 17

Overview Of Bison Ranching 17

Historical Background And Evolution 18

Benefits Of Raising Bison 19

Key Differences between Bison And Cattle 20

Essential Terms And Definitions................. 22

Herd: 22

Forage: 22

Cull: 22

Range: 22

CHAPTER TWO 25

Setting Up Your Bison Ranch 25

Choosing The Right Location 25

Land And Pasture Requirements 26

Fencing And Facilities 28

Water Supply And Management 29

Equipment And Infrastructure Needs 30

CHAPTER THREE 33

Selecting Bison For Your Ranch 33

Types Of Bison Breeds 33

   1. Plains Bison: 33

   2. Wood Bison: 33

   3. Hybrid Bison: 34

Criteria For Selecting Healthy Bison 34

   1. Physical Health: 34

   2. Genetic Background: 34

   3. Temperament: 35

   4. Reproductive Health: 35

Understanding Bison Genetics 35

   1. Genetic Diversity: 36

- 2. Inbreeding Risks: 36
- 3. Selective Breeding: 36

Buying Bison: Where And How 36
- 1. Finding Suppliers: 37
- 2. Inspecting Animals: 37
- 3. Negotiating Terms: 37

Record-Keeping And Tracking 37
- 1. Health Records: 38
- 2. Breeding Records: 38
- 3. Financial Records: 38
- 4. Inventory Management: 38

CHAPTER FOUR 41

Bison Nutrition And Feeding 41

Essential Dietary Requirements 41

Types Of Feed And Supplements 42

Grazing Vs. Supplemental Feeding 44

Managing Pasture And Forage 45

Seasonal Feeding Considerations 46

CHAPTER FIVE 49

Health And Veterinary Care 49

Common Bison Diseases And Issues 49

Routine Health Checks And Vaccinations 51

Establishing A Veterinary Care Plan 53

Managing Injuries And Emergencies 56

Biosecurity Measures 58

CHAPTER SIX 61

Breeding And Reproduction 61

Understanding Bison Reproduction 61

    Basic Reproductive Physiology: 62

    Breeding Season and Rut: 62

    Gestation and Calving: 62

Breeding Management Strategies 63

Selective Breeding: 63

Bull-to-Cow Ratio: 63

Artificial Insemination: 64

Pregnancy And Birthing Process 64

Pregnancy Diagnosis: 64

Birthing Management: 65

Calf Care And Weaning 65

Immediate Care: 65

Weaning: 66

Record-Keeping For Breeding 66

Data Collection: 66

Analysis and Decision-Making: 67

CHAPTER SEVEN 69

Bison Behavior And Handling 69

Understanding Bison Behavior 69

Safe Handling And Interaction Techniques ... 70

Training And Taming Methods 72

Behavior Management Strategies 73

Building Trust With Bison 74

CHAPTER EIGHT 77

Marketing And Selling Bison Products 77

Market Research And Opportunities 77

Processing And Packaging Bison Meat 79

Promoting Bison Products 80

Pricing Strategies 82

Legal And Regulatory Considerations 83

CHAPTER NINE 85

Financial Management And Planning 85

Budgeting And Cost Estimation 85

Financial Record-Keeping 86

Investment And Funding Options 88

Profitability Analysis 89

Risk Management Strategies 90

CHAPTER TEN 93

Sustainability And Future Trends 93

Sustainable Bison Ranching Practices 93

Environmental Impact Considerations 95

Innovations In Bison Farming 96

Adapting To Market Changes 98

Planning For Long-Term Success 99

Frequently Asked Question And Answers 101

CONCLUSION 108

THE END 112

ABOUT THIS BOOK

"Bison Ranching" serves as an indispensable resource for anyone interested in this unique and rewarding agricultural endeavor. This comprehensive guide offers a deep dive into the multifaceted world of bison ranching, from its historical roots to contemporary practices and future possibilities.

This book begins by providing a thorough overview of bison ranching, including its historical evolution and the myriad benefits of raising bison. It elucidates the key differences between bison and cattle, introducing essential terms and concepts to ensure a solid foundation for readers new to the field.

Setting up a bison ranch is a complex undertaking, and this book addresses it in detail. It covers the critical aspects of selecting the right location, understanding land and pasture requirements, and establishing the necessary fencing and facilities.

It also delves into water supply management and the essential equipment needed to maintain a functional ranch.

Selecting the right bison is crucial for a successful ranching operation. This book explores various bison breeds, offers criteria for choosing healthy animals, and explains the intricacies of bison genetics. It also guides readers through the process of buying bison, including where to find them and how to keep accurate records for effective tracking.

Feeding bison properly is essential for their health and productivity. This guide addresses the dietary needs of bison, including the types of feed and supplements they require. It also covers the differences between grazing and supplemental feeding, pasture management, and seasonal feeding considerations to ensure optimal nutrition throughout the year.

Health and veterinary care are paramount in bison ranching. This book provides valuable insights into common bison diseases, routine health checks, and vaccination schedules. It also includes advice on establishing a veterinary care plan, managing injuries and emergencies, and implementing biosecurity measures to protect the herd.

Breeding and reproduction are vital components of a successful bison ranch. This guide covers the fundamentals of bison reproduction, including breeding management strategies, pregnancy, and the birthing process. It also addresses calf care, weaning, and the importance of record-keeping for effective breeding programs.

Understanding bison behavior is key to successful ranching. This book offers strategies for safe handling, training, and taming bison. It emphasizes the importance of building trust with these animals and managing their behavior to foster a productive and harmonious ranch environment.

Marketing and selling bison products are crucial for profitability. This book provides insights into market research, processing, and packaging of bison meat, and effective promotion strategies. It also covers pricing, legal, and regulatory considerations to help ranchers successfully navigate the commercial landscape.

Financial management is an integral part of running a bison ranch. The guide includes practical advice on budgeting, cost estimation, and financial record-keeping. It explores investment and funding options, profitability analysis, and risk management strategies to ensure long-term financial stability.

Finally, This book addresses sustainability and future trends in bison ranching. It discusses sustainable practices, environmental impact, and innovations in bison farming. It also guides adapting to market changes and planning for long-term success to keep the ranching operation thriving well into the future.

Overall, "Bison Ranching" is an essential manual for both aspiring and seasoned ranchers, offering a wealth of knowledge and practical advice to help them succeed in this rewarding field.

CHAPTER ONE

Introduction To Bison Ranching

Overview Of Bison Ranching

Bison ranching involves the farming and management of bison for meat, hides, and other products. Unlike traditional cattle ranching, bison ranching offers a unique set of challenges and benefits. Bison are robust and resilient animals that thrive in a variety of climates, making them an excellent choice for diverse ranching environments. They require less intensive management compared to cattle, which can result in lower operational costs.

When starting a bison ranch, it's important to understand the specific needs of bison, including their dietary requirements, space, and social behavior.

Bison are herd animals and need ample space to roam and graze. They also require a diet that includes high-quality forage and sometimes supplemental feed. Bison are generally hardy animals, but they do need proper shelter and water sources. Setting up a bison ranch involves careful planning and investment in appropriate infrastructure to ensure the health and productivity of the herd.

Historical Background And Evolution

Bison have been a part of North American ecosystems for thousands of years. Historically, they were central to the livelihoods of many Indigenous peoples, who relied on bison for food, clothing, and tools. The bison population was decimated in the 19th century due to overhunting and habitat loss, leading to near extinction by the early 1900s.

Conservation efforts began in the late 1800s, leading to the establishment of bison ranches to help restore and preserve the species.

Modern bison ranching evolved from these conservation efforts, with a focus on sustainable management and commercial production. Today, bison ranching not only supports conservation but also provides economic opportunities for ranchers. The industry has grown as demand for bison meat and products has increased, driven by consumer interest in healthier, leaner alternatives to traditional beef. Understanding this historical context helps ranchers appreciate the significance of their work and the importance of maintaining sustainable practices.

Benefits Of Raising Bison

Raising bison offers numerous benefits, both for ranchers and consumers. One of the main advantages is the meat's nutritional profile. Bison meat is leaner and lower in fat compared to beef, and it contains higher levels of beneficial nutrients such as omega-3 fatty acids and vitamin B12. This makes it an attractive option for health-conscious consumers.

Bison are also well-suited to a range of environments, including harsher climates where other livestock might struggle. Their natural hardiness means they are less susceptible to some diseases and parasites that affect cattle, reducing the need for medical interventions. Additionally, bison are often considered more environmentally friendly than traditional cattle due to their grazing patterns, which can help maintain soil health and biodiversity.

Key Differences between Bison And Cattle

Understanding the differences between bison and cattle is crucial for successful bison ranching. One of the most notable differences is their physical characteristics. Bison are larger and more muscular than cattle, with a distinctive hump over their shoulders and a thick coat that provides insulation against cold weather. This unique appearance affects their handling and management, requiring different approaches compared to cattle.

Behaviorally, bison are more aggressive and unpredictable than cattle, especially during mating season or when they feel threatened. This means ranchers need to be cautious and well-prepared when working with bison. Additionally, bison are generally more independent and less reliant on human intervention than cattle, which can be both an advantage and a challenge depending on the ranching goals. For example, their tendency to roam and graze extensively can lead to more complex fencing and pasture management needs.

Essential Terms And Definitions

To navigate the world of bison ranching, it's important to understand some key terms and definitions. Here are a few essential terms:

Herd: A group of bison that live and graze together. Herd management involves understanding their social structure and behavior.

Forage: Plant material that bison graze on. High-quality forage is essential for their nutrition and overall health.

Cull: The process of removing certain animals from the herd, often due to age, health, or breeding goals.

Range: The area of land where bison graze and live. Proper range management is crucial for maintaining healthy bison and land.

Understanding these terms helps ranchers effectively communicate and manage their bison herds, ensuring that they can address issues promptly and efficiently.

CHAPTER TWO

Setting Up Your Bison Ranch

Choosing The Right Location

Selecting the optimal location for your bison ranch is crucial for the health of your herd and the success of your operation. Bison are adaptable animals, but they thrive best in environments that mimic their native habitat. Ideal locations are generally characterized by expansive, open spaces with minimal human interference. Look for areas with a climate that provides a good balance of hot summers and cold winters, as bison are well-suited to a range of temperatures.

When choosing a location, consider the soil quality and drainage. Bison are heavy animals, and poor drainage can lead to muddy conditions, which may cause health issues.

A site with well-draining soil and proper grading will help prevent such problems. Additionally, the area should have access to natural vegetation, as bison prefer grazing on grasses and plants that are part of their natural diet.

Finally, proximity to veterinary services and feed suppliers is important. While bison can often forage for much of their diet, having reliable access to supplemental feed and healthcare services will help ensure your herd remains in good condition. Assess the accessibility of roads and transport options, as this will be crucial for managing deliveries and any necessary travel for your bison.

Land And Pasture Requirements

Bison require ample space to roam, graze, and exhibit their natural behaviors. A general guideline is to provide at least 1 to 2 acres of pasture per bison, but this can vary based on the quality of the land and the density of vegetation. The pasture should consist of a mix of grasses and legumes, which provide essential nutrients and help maintain a healthy diet for the bison. Avoid overgrazing by rotating pastures to allow for regrowth and prevent soil degradation.

Proper land management is key to maintaining productive pastures. Regularly assess the condition of your pastures, and reseed or amended the soil as needed to ensure optimal growth. Implementing a rotational grazing system can help improve pasture health and reduce the risk of disease. This involves dividing your pasture into smaller sections and moving the bison between them periodically to allow rest and recovery for each section.

Consider incorporating additional forage options such as supplemental hay or silage during winter months or periods of drought when pasture growth may be limited.

This will ensure that your bison have a consistent food source and prevent nutritional deficiencies.

Fencing And Facilities

Effective fencing is essential for bison ranching due to the size and strength of these animals. Bison are known for their ability to challenge and breach fences, so sturdy, high-quality fencing is a must. A common recommendation is to use a combination of barbed wire and electric fencing to create a barrier that is both secure and visible to the bison. The fence should be at least 5 to 6 feet tall and well-maintained to prevent escapes.

In addition to fencing, you will need to establish various facilities to support the daily operations of your ranch. This includes handling facilities such as corrals, chutes, and loading ramps for managing and moving the bison safely. These structures should be built to withstand the force and weight of bison and should be designed to minimize stress on the animals during handling.

Shelters are also important to protect bison from extreme weather conditions. While bison are hardy and can tolerate cold and heat, having access to shaded or covered areas helps reduce the risk of weather-related stress. Ensure that shelters are well-ventilated and large enough to accommodate all bison comfortably.

Water Supply And Management

A reliable water supply is critical for bison health and productivity. Bison require a significant amount of water daily, so it is essential to provide access to clean, fresh water at all times. Depending on the size of your ranch and the number of bison, you may need to install water troughs or ponds. Ensure that water sources are regularly cleaned and maintained to prevent contamination.

Water management involves not only providing access but also ensuring that the water supply is sufficient throughout the year. During dry periods or winter months, supplement natural water sources with additional troughs or heaters to prevent freezing. Regularly check the water levels and quality to address any issues promptly.

Consider implementing a water conservation plan to optimize water use and minimize waste. This can include strategies such as rainwater harvesting or using efficient watering systems that reduce water runoff and evaporation. Effective water management contributes to the overall health of your bison and the sustainability of your ranching operation.

Equipment And Infrastructure Needs

Equipping your bison ranch with the right tools and infrastructure is vital for efficient operation. Essential equipment includes vehicles for transporting feed and bison, as well as tools for maintaining fences and handling facilities. Depending on the scale of your ranch, you may also need machinery for pasture management, such as mowers, seeders, and fertilizer spreaders.

Infrastructure requirements include buildings for storing feed, equipment, and other supplies. Ensure that these structures are well-ventilated and secure to protect against pests and weather conditions. Additionally, consider setting up a workshop for maintenance and repairs of equipment and facilities.

Investing in technology can also enhance your ranching operations. This might include automated feeding systems, monitoring equipment for tracking bison health and behavior, and record-keeping software to manage your herd's data effectively. By integrating these tools, you can streamline operations and improve overall efficiency on your bison ranch.

CHAPTER THREE

Selecting Bison For Your Ranch

Types Of Bison Breeds

Bison ranching begins with understanding the various breeds available, each with unique characteristics suited to different environments and purposes. The most common breeds include:

1.	Plains Bison: Known for their hardiness and adaptability, Plains Bison are the most widespread breed in North America. They thrive in open grasslands and are valued for their robust health and meat quality.

2.	Wood Bison: Larger and more robust than Plains Bison, Wood Bison are adapted to colder climates and dense forests.

They require more space and specialized handling due to their size but are valued for their resilience and genetic diversity.

3. Hybrid Bison: Some ranchers breed hybrids, combining the best traits of Plains and Wood Bison to suit specific ranching conditions or market demands. Hybrid bison often exhibit a blend of characteristics from both parent breeds.

Criteria For Selecting Healthy Bison

Choosing healthy bison is crucial for a successful ranching operation. Key criteria to consider include:

1. Physical Health: Look for bison with clear eyes, a shiny coat, and alert behavior. Avoid animals showing signs of lameness, excessive scratching, or dull fur, as these may indicate health issues.

2. Genetic Background: Assess the bison's genetic lineage to understand potential health risks and desirable traits. Breeding from healthy, genetically diverse animals improves overall herd vitality and productivity.

3. Temperament: A calm temperament is essential for handling and managing bison safely. Avoid aggressive or overly skittish animals, as they can pose safety risks to both handlers and other bison.

4. Reproductive Health: If purchasing breeding stock, ensure the bison has a history of successful breeding and calving. Check reproductive records and consult with breeders or veterinarians to verify fertility and reproductive health.

Understanding Bison Genetics

Bison genetics play a crucial role in herd management and breeding programs. Key aspects to understand include:

1. Genetic Diversity: Maintaining a diverse gene pool reduces the risk of genetic disorders and enhances herd resilience against diseases and environmental challenges.

2. Inbreeding Risks: Avoid excessive inbreeding, which can lead to genetic defects and reduced fertility. Implement genetic testing and breeding strategies that promote genetic diversity.

3. Selective Breeding: Select desirable traits such as meat quality, size, and resistance to specific diseases. Breeding programs should aim to improve herd genetics while preserving valuable traits unique to bison.

Buying Bison: Where And How

When purchasing bison for your ranch, consider the following steps:

1. **Finding Suppliers:** Research reputable bison breeders or auctions known for high-quality stock. Attend bison auctions or contact breed associations to connect with reliable sellers.

2. **Inspecting Animals:** Personally inspect potential purchases to assess their health, temperament, and suitability for your ranching goals. Ask for health certificates and genetic records from the seller.

3. **Negotiating Terms:** Discuss pricing, delivery options, and any guarantees or warranties offered by the seller. Clarify transport arrangements and ensure proper handling during transit to minimize stress on the animals.

Record-Keeping And Tracking

Effective record-keeping is essential for managing a successful bison ranch. Key aspects include:

1. **Health Records:** Maintain detailed records of vaccinations, treatments, and health checks for each bison. This helps track individual health histories and ensure timely medical interventions.

2. **Breeding Records:** Record breeding dates, birth records, and genetic information to monitor reproductive success and lineage. This data aids in making informed breeding decisions and improving herd genetics over time.

3. **Financial Records:** Track expenses related to feed, veterinary care, and infrastructure maintenance. Budgeting and financial planning rely on accurate cost data to optimize ranch operations.

4. **Inventory Management:** Regularly update inventory records to track herd size, individual animal status, and changes in herd composition due to births, deaths, or sales.

By maintaining comprehensive records, ranchers can enhance herd management, improve breeding outcomes, and ensure the overall health and productivity of their bison operation.

CHAPTER FOUR

Bison Nutrition And Feeding

Essential Dietary Requirements

Bison, like other large herbivores, have specific nutritional needs that are crucial for their health and productivity. Understanding these requirements is key to successful bison ranching. Bison primarily needs a balanced diet consisting of carbohydrates, proteins, vitamins, and minerals.

Carbohydrates are essential for energy. Bison derive their carbohydrate needs mainly from fibrous plant material like grasses and hay. The quality of the forage impacts their energy levels and overall health. Proteins are vital for growth and reproduction. Bison require high-quality protein sources, which are found in legumes and protein-rich forages.

Minerals such as calcium and phosphorus are needed for bone development and metabolic functions. A mineral supplement may be necessary to ensure bison get adequate levels, especially if the natural forage is deficient.

Additionally, vitamins, particularly vitamins A and E, play important roles in maintaining immune function and overall health. Forage can be supplemented with vitamin-rich feeds if the natural diet is lacking. Ensuring that bison have access to clean water at all times is also crucial for their health and digestion.

Types Of Feed And Supplements

When it comes to feeding bison, a variety of feed types and supplements are available. The choice of feed depends on factors such as the bison's age, weight, and purpose (e.g., breeding, meat production).

Forage is the primary feed, and it includes grasses, legumes, and hay. High-quality hay should be free of mold and contaminants to ensure it meets nutritional standards.

Grain supplements such as corn or barley can be used to provide additional energy, especially during periods when forage quality is low. Protein supplements like soybean meal or alfalfa pellets may be added to boost protein intake, which is important for growth and reproduction. Additionally, mineral supplements in the form of blocks or loose minerals can help prevent deficiencies and support overall health.

Salt licks are also beneficial, as they provide essential minerals that may be missing from the bison's diet. The supplement choice should be tailored to the specific needs of the bison and should be adjusted based on regular nutritional assessments.

Grazing Vs. Supplemental Feeding

Bison are natural grazers and thrive on a diet of high-quality pasture. Grazing allows bison to consume a variety of forages and helps them maintain natural eating behaviors. However, grazing alone may not always provide all the necessary nutrients, especially during certain times of the year or if the pasture is of poor quality.

Supplemental feeding can be crucial during periods when pasture growth is insufficient, such as winter or drought conditions. Providing supplemental feed helps ensure that bison receive adequate nutrition when natural forage is limited. The type and amount of supplements should be based on nutritional analysis and the specific needs of the herd.

Balancing grazing with supplemental feeding requires careful planning. Ideally, bison should have access to high-quality pasture and be supplemented only as needed. Monitoring the health and condition of the herd can help determine when and how much supplemental feed to provide.

Managing Pasture And Forage

Effective pasture and forage management are essential for maintaining a healthy bison herd. Pasture management involves rotating grazing areas to prevent overgrazing and allow for the recovery of forage plants. This practice helps maintain soil health and improves forage quality.

Forage quality can be managed by planting and maintaining high-nutrient grasses and legumes that are suited to the local climate. Regular soil testing can help determine the need for fertilization or lime applications to improve soil fertility and forage production.

Pasture renovation may be necessary if the land becomes degraded. This can involve reseeding or planting new forage species that are more resilient or better suited to the soil conditions. Ensuring that pastures are well-managed helps provide bison with a consistent and nutritious food supply.

Seasonal Feeding Considerations

Seasonal changes can significantly impact the nutritional needs of bison. During summer, bison generally have access to abundant and high-quality forage. However, winter presents challenges as forage quality declines and may become less available.

In winter, bison may require supplemental feeding to meet their nutritional needs. Providing high-quality hay and possibly grain supplements can help ensure they receive adequate energy and nutrients. Spring and fall are transitional periods where pasture conditions and forage quality can vary, necessitating adjustments in feeding strategies.

Monitoring bison during these seasonal changes and adjusting their diet accordingly is key to maintaining their health and productivity. Keeping detailed records of feed intake and bison condition can help in making informed decisions about seasonal feeding practices.

CHAPTER FIVE

Health And Veterinary Care

Common Bison Diseases And Issues

Bison, like any livestock, are susceptible to various diseases and health issues that can affect their well-being and productivity. Understanding these common ailments is crucial for effective ranch management.

1. Common Diseases Bison may encounter several diseases, including:

Brucellosis: A bacterial infection causing reproductive issues.

Anthrax: Often fatal bacterial infection affecting multiple organs.

Bovine Tuberculosis: Respiratory disease that can spread to other animals.

Foot Rot: Bacterial infection causing lameness and hoof issues.

Each disease requires specific management strategies and may involve quarantine measures to prevent spread.

2. Health Issues Apart from diseases, bison can face health challenges such as:

Parasitic Infections: Including internal parasites like worms.

Nutritional Deficiencies: Resulting from inadequate diets.

Heat Stress: Especially problematic in hot climates.

Addressing these issues involves regular monitoring, dietary adjustments, and ensuring adequate shelter and cooling during hot periods.

3. Management Practices Implementing a robust health management plan is essential:

Regular Monitoring: Routine health checks for signs of illness or distress.

Vaccination Programs: Administering vaccines against prevalent diseases.

Dietary Supplements: Providing minerals and vitamins to prevent deficiencies.

By staying vigilant and proactive, ranchers can maintain bison health and minimize the impact of diseases and health issues.

Routine Health Checks And Vaccinations

To ensure the well-being of bison herds, regular health checks and vaccinations are imperative.

1. Health Checks Conduct thorough health checks:

Physical Examination: Assessing body condition, signs of illness, and injuries.

Behavioral Observations: Monitoring eating habits, mobility, and social interactions.

Parasite Testing: Regular fecal exams to detect internal parasites.

Early detection allows prompt treatment and prevents the spread of diseases within the herd.

2. Vaccination Programs Establish a vaccination schedule:

Core Vaccines: Protect against diseases like brucellosis and clostridial infections.

Optional Vaccines: Consider additional vaccines based on regional disease risks.

Administer vaccines according to manufacturer guidelines and consult with a veterinarian for tailored recommendations.

3. Record Keeping Maintain detailed health records:

Vaccination Dates: Documenting vaccine type, batch numbers, and expiration dates.

Health History: Recording illnesses, treatments, and outcomes.

Observations: Noting any abnormalities or changes in herd health.

Accurate records aid in tracking health trends, assessing vaccine efficacy, and informing future management decisions.

Establishing A Veterinary Care Plan

Creating a veterinary care plan ensures timely intervention and optimal health outcomes for bison.

1. Veterinary Relationships Forge partnerships with veterinarians:

Emergency Contact: Establishing 24/7 availability for urgent situations.

Consultations: Seeking advice on health issues and treatment options.

Training: Educating staff on basic first aid and emergency response.

Collaboration with veterinarians enhances herd health management and readiness for medical emergencies.

2. Emergency Preparedness Prepare for unforeseen health crises:

Emergency Kit: Stocking supplies for wound care, medication administration, and immobilization.

Protocols: Developing protocols for handling injuries, illnesses, and evacuations.

Training: Conduct drills to practice emergency responses and enhance team proficiency.

Efficient emergency preparedness minimizes downtime and mitigates health risks during critical situations.

3. Continuous Improvement Evaluate and refine the care plan:

Feedback Loop: Soliciting input from veterinarians, staff, and stakeholders.

Performance Review: Assessing plan effectiveness and adapting to evolving health challenges.

Education: Keeping abreast of advancements in veterinary medicine and management practices.

Continuous improvement ensures proactive healthcare delivery and optimizes bison welfare over time.

Managing Injuries And Emergencies

Timely intervention is essential in managing bison injuries and emergencies to minimize health risks and ensure rapid recovery.

1. Injury Assessment Promptly assess injuries:

Severity: Determining the extent of trauma or wounds.

Location: Identifying injuries affecting mobility or vital functions.

Immediate Care: Providing first aid to stabilize the injured animal.

Early intervention prevents complications and facilitates effective treatment strategies.

2. Treatment Protocols Implement treatment procedures:

Wound Care: Cleaning, disinfecting, and dressing wounds to prevent infection.

Pain Management: Administering analgesics to alleviate discomfort and aid recovery.

Rest and Rehabilitation: Providing supportive care for injured bison during recovery.

Following established protocols promotes healing and restores health following injuries.

3. Follow-up Care Monitor recovery progress:

Observation: Monitoring behavior, appetite, and wound healing.

Veterinary Consultation: Seeking follow-up care and adjusting treatment as needed.

Reintegration: Gradually reintroducing healed bison to the herd environment.

Comprehensive follow-up ensures complete recovery and minimizes the risk of recurrence or complications.

Biosecurity Measures

Biosecurity protocols are critical in preventing disease introduction and transmission within bison herds.

1. Biosecurity Planning Develop a biosecurity strategy:

Risk Assessment: Identifying potential sources of disease introduction.

Quarantine Procedures: Isolating new arrivals and animals returning from external environments.

Visitor Policies: Restricting farm access and implementing visitor hygiene protocols.

Strict biosecurity measures safeguard herd health and maintain operational continuity.

2. Facility Management Optimize farm infrastructure:

Separation Zones: Establishing buffer areas between different herd groups.

Sanitation Practices: Disinfecting equipment, vehicles, and shared facilities regularly.

Pest Control: Managing vectors that can transmit diseases to bison.

Maintaining a clean and controlled environment minimizes disease risks and enhances herd immunity.

3. Education and Training Promote biosecurity awareness:

Staff Training: Educating personnel on biosecurity protocols and disease prevention.

Communication: Informing stakeholders, visitors, and suppliers about biosecurity expectations.

Continuous Review: Updating protocols based on emerging threats and industry best practices.

Active engagement ensures collective responsibility for biosecurity and protects bison health in the long term.

CHAPTER SIX

Breeding And Reproduction

Understanding Bison Reproduction

Bison reproduction is crucial for sustaining a successful ranching operation. Understanding the basics of bison reproductive biology is essential for effective breeding management. Bison are typically polygamous animals, with males (bulls) competing for dominance and mating opportunities during the rutting season. Bulls exhibit various mating behaviors, including vocalizations, wallowing in mud, and sometimes engaging in physical contests to establish dominance.

Basic Reproductive Physiology: Bison cows (females) reach sexual maturity at around two to three years old, although some may mature slightly earlier or later. The estrous cycle of a bison cow lasts approximately 21 days, during which she is receptive to mating for about 12 to 18 hours. Bulls detect receptive cows through olfactory cues and behaviors such as sniffing and trailing. Once a bull identifies a receptive cow, mating occurs through copulation, which can last from a few minutes to half an hour.

Breeding Season and Rut: The breeding season, or rut, typically occurs in late summer to early autumn. During this period, testosterone levels in bulls rise, triggering aggressive behaviors and mating activity. Ranchers often monitor the herd closely during rut to ensure optimal breeding outcomes.

Gestation and Calving: Bison have a gestation period of approximately 9 months (approximately 270 days).

Pregnancy diagnosis can be challenging without specialized equipment, often relying on behavioral cues and observation.

Calving generally occurs in late spring or early summer when conditions are favorable for calf survival. Bison calves are precocial, meaning they are relatively mature and mobile shortly after birth.

Breeding Management Strategies

Effective breeding management is vital for maximizing reproductive success and herd health.

Selective Breeding: Ranchers may employ selective breeding to enhance desirable traits such as size, temperament, and disease resistance within their herd. This involves carefully choosing breeding stock based on genetic potential and performance.

Bull-to-Cow Ratio: Maintaining an appropriate bull-to-cow ratio is crucial during breeding season to ensure adequate mating opportunities without causing excessive stress or injury among the bulls.

A ratio of one bull to 20-30 cows is typically recommended to optimize breeding efficiency.

Artificial Insemination: Some ranchers may opt for artificial insemination to introduce specific genetics into their herd or overcome breeding challenges. This technique involves collecting semen from high-quality bulls and artificially inseminating selected cows during their estrus cycle.

Pregnancy And Birthing Process

Managing pregnancy and parturition (birthing) is critical for ensuring the health and survival of both cow and calf.

Pregnancy Diagnosis: While challenging without advanced equipment, pregnancy can sometimes be confirmed through behavioral changes and physical observations.

Veterinarians or experienced ranchers may perform palpation or ultrasound for a more accurate diagnosis.

Birthing Management: Bison cows typically give birth without human intervention, preferring secluded areas within the ranch. However, monitoring pregnant cows closely as their due date approaches allows ranchers to assist if necessary. Bison calves are relatively large at birth and require minimal assistance in most cases.

Calf Care And Weaning

Proper calf care is essential for ensuring healthy growth and development.

Immediate Care: Upon birth, bison calves should be monitored to ensure they can stand and nurse properly. Colostrum intake within the first hours of life is crucial for immune system development.

Weaning: Bison calves are naturally weaned by their mothers between six to ten months of age. Ranchers may separate calves from cows gradually to minimize stress and ensure proper nutrition during the weaning process.

Record-Keeping For Breeding

Maintaining accurate records is key to effective breeding management and herd improvement.

Data Collection: Ranchers should record breeding dates, bull assignments, pregnancy diagnosis results, calving dates, and calf health information. This data helps track individual animal performance, genetic lines, and overall herd productivity.

Analysis and Decision-Making: Analyzing breeding records allows ranchers to make informed decisions regarding bull selection, breeding strategies, and herd health management. Regular review and adjustment of breeding plans based on performance data contribute to long-term herd improvement.

CHAPTER SEVEN

Bison Behavior And Handling

Understanding Bison Behavior

Bison are large, powerful animals with complex behaviors influenced by their instincts and social structure. Understanding bison behavior is crucial for successful ranching, as it helps in predicting their actions and ensuring safe interaction. Bison are inherently herd animals with a strong sense of hierarchy. This means they often follow the lead of dominant individuals, which can influence their behavior in various situations.

In the wild, bison exhibit a range of behaviors based on their need for food, safety, and social interaction. They graze in large groups and migrate in response to seasonal changes.

On a ranch, these natural behaviors manifest in their interactions with other bison and humans. Recognizing signs of stress, aggression, or contentment can help ranchers manage their herds effectively. For example, bison may display signs of agitation such as snorting or pawing the ground if they feel threatened or uncomfortable.

Behavioral patterns also vary between males and females. Males often show more aggressive behavior, especially during mating season, while females are more social and nurturing. Understanding these differences allows ranchers to tailor their handling practices to the specific needs of each gender, ensuring a safer and more productive environment.

Safe Handling And Interaction Techniques

Handling bison requires careful planning and a thorough understanding of their behavior. Safety is paramount, as bison are powerful and can be unpredictable. The first step in safe handling is to establish a proper handling facility, including sturdy fencing and safe working areas. Fences should be at least 6 to 8 feet high, as bison are known to jump and test boundaries.

When interacting with bison, it's essential to use low-stress techniques that minimize fear and aggression. Approach bison slowly and from the side rather than head-on, which can be perceived as a threat. Maintain a calm and assertive demeanor to avoid startling the animals. Using appropriate equipment such as chutes and corrals designed for bison can also facilitate safe handling. Ensure that all equipment is in good condition and free from hazards that could injure the animals or handlers.

It's beneficial to have a clear plan for handling bison during routine activities such as vaccinations or branding. This involves having trained personnel who understand bison behavior and can execute handling procedures efficiently. Practice and preparation help reduce the stress on the animals and improve overall safety during these operations.

Training And Taming Methods

Training bison requires patience and consistency. Unlike domesticated animals, bison are not naturally inclined to follow commands, so building a relationship based on trust is essential. Start by familiarizing bison with human presence and gradually introduce them to handling procedures. This can be done by spending time near the animals, allowing them to become accustomed to human activity without direct interaction.

Positive reinforcement is a powerful tool in training bison. Offering food rewards or treats can encourage desirable behaviors and create a positive association with human interaction. For instance, feeding bison from a trough or hand can help them associate humans with positive experiences, making them more receptive to handling over time.

It's important to avoid punitive methods or sudden movements, as these can increase stress and lead to defensive behavior. Instead, use gentle, repetitive training sessions to reinforce desired behaviors. Over time, bison will become more comfortable with handling and may even exhibit more cooperative behavior during routine management tasks.

Behavior Management Strategies

Effective behavior management involves understanding and addressing the root causes of problematic behaviors. For example, aggression in bison can often be traced to factors such as overcrowding, inadequate resources, or perceived threats. Identifying these triggers and making adjustments to the environment or management practices can help mitigate aggressive behavior.

Regular observation and monitoring of the herd allow ranchers to detect early signs of behavioral issues. Keeping detailed records of bison behavior and any changes in their environment can help identify patterns and potential solutions. Implementing strategies such as rotational grazing or providing additional enrichment can address issues related to boredom or stress.

Additionally, working with experienced bison handlers or behaviorists can provide valuable insights and techniques for managing complex behaviors. These professionals can offer tailored advice based on their expertise, helping ranchers develop effective strategies for maintaining a harmonious and productive herd.

Building Trust With Bison

Building trust with bison is a gradual process that requires consistency and respect. Establishing a positive relationship starts with regular, nonthreatening interactions. Spend time near the bison without attempting to handle them initially, allowing them to become accustomed to your presence.

Use calm, consistent body language and voice when interacting with bison. Avoid sudden movements or loud noises that could startle them. Offering food and engaging in gentle, repetitive activities helps create a sense of familiarity and trust. For example, regularly feeding bison from the same location can help them associate you with positive experiences.

Over time, as bison become more comfortable with human interaction, you can gradually introduce handling procedures. Continue to use positive reinforcement to encourage cooperation and build a stronger bond. Patience and respect are key to developing a trusting relationship with bison, ultimately leading to more effective and stress-free management.

CHAPTER EIGHT

Marketing And Selling Bison Products

Market Research And Opportunities

Market research is a critical first step in successfully marketing and selling bison products. Begin by understanding the current market demand for bison meat and other bison products. This involves gathering data on consumer preferences, identifying target demographics, and analyzing competition. Start with online research to find existing bison producers and their market strategies. Look into industry reports, market trends, and consumer surveys to gauge the popularity of bison products in different regions.

Next, conduct local surveys and focus groups to understand your potential customers' tastes and purchasing habits. Visit farmer's markets, specialty meat stores, and restaurants to gather insights on current consumer interest and demand. You may also want to reach out to local chefs and food critics for their opinions on bison meat. Networking within agricultural and meat industry associations can provide valuable information about market opportunities and emerging trends.

Identify niche markets and potential selling points for bison products. These may include health-conscious consumers who prefer leaner meats, gourmet food enthusiasts, or sustainable food advocates. By targeting specific segments, you can tailor your marketing efforts and product offerings to meet their needs and preferences, thus maximizing your market potential.

Processing And Packaging Bison Meat

Processing bison meat requires adherence to specific guidelines to ensure safety, quality, and compliance with regulations. Begin by selecting a licensed processing facility or setting up your own if you meet the requirements. The processing process includes butchering the bison, which involves skinning, removing internal organs, and cutting the meat into various cuts.

Once the meat is processed, it must be packaged correctly to maintain freshness and quality. Use vacuum-sealing technology to remove air and prevent freezer burn. Label each package with information such as the cut of meat, weight, processing date, and any relevant nutritional information.

Ensure your packaging complies with local regulations, which may require specific labeling for meat products.

To maintain high standards of hygiene and quality, implement a stringent cleaning and sanitation protocol for your processing area. Regularly inspect and maintain equipment to ensure it operates efficiently and safely. Employ trained personnel who follow best practices in meat handling and processing to minimize contamination and ensure top-quality products.

Promoting Bison Products

Effective promotion of bison products involves a strategic marketing approach. Start by creating a strong brand identity that reflects the unique qualities of bison meat. Develop a professional logo, website, and marketing materials that convey the premium nature of your products.

Utilize social media platforms to build a following and engage with potential customers. Share informative content about the benefits of bison meat, recipes, and behind-the-scenes looks at your operation.

Participate in local food events, farmers' markets, and trade shows to showcase your products and connect with consumers. Offer samples to allow potential buyers to experience the taste and quality of bison meat firsthand. Collaborate with local chefs and restaurants to feature bison dishes on their menus, which can increase visibility and drive interest in your products.

Leverage partnerships with health and wellness influencers or food bloggers to promote your bison products. Provide them with samples and information to share with their audience. This can help expand your reach and attract customers who are interested in healthier meat options or unique culinary experiences.

Pricing Strategies

Setting the right price for bison products involves considering various factors to ensure profitability while remaining competitive. Begin by analyzing your production costs, including the costs of raising, processing, and packaging bison meat. Factor in overhead expenses such as facility maintenance, labor, and marketing costs. Ensure that your pricing covers these costs while allowing for a reasonable profit margin.

Research the pricing of similar products in your target market to gauge the going rates for bison meat. Position your prices competitively based on the quality and uniqueness of your products. Consider offering different pricing tiers for various cuts of meat or value-added products such as bison jerky or sausages.

Implement promotional pricing strategies to attract customers and drive sales. This could include offering discounts for bulk purchases, seasonal promotions, or introductory offers for new customers. Monitor the impact of these pricing strategies on your sales and adjust as needed to optimize revenue and customer satisfaction.

Legal And Regulatory Considerations

Complying with legal and regulatory requirements is essential for operating a bison ranch and selling bison products. Start by understanding federal, state, and local regulations related to livestock management, meat processing, and food safety. Obtain necessary licenses and permits for processing and selling bison meat, and ensure that your processing facility meets all regulatory standards.

Follow guidelines for meat inspection and labeling, which may include requirements for hygiene practices, temperature control, and record-keeping. Work with a food safety consultant or regulatory agency to ensure that your processes adhere to industry standards and regulations.

Stay informed about changes in regulations and industry best practices to ensure ongoing compliance. Regularly review and update your operational procedures to address any new legal requirements or changes in food safety standards. This will help you avoid potential legal issues and maintain a reputation for quality and reliability in the market.

CHAPTER NINE

Financial Management And Planning

Budgeting And Cost Estimation

Budgeting and cost estimation are fundamental aspects of financial management in bison ranching. To start, it's crucial to outline all potential expenses and income sources. Begin by identifying fixed costs such as land, facilities, equipment, and labor. Fixed costs are consistent and necessary for daily operations. For example, consider the expenses for purchasing and maintaining fencing, feeding systems, and housing for the bison.

Next, calculate variable costs, which fluctuate based on the size of the herd and market conditions. These include feed, veterinary services, and transportation. To estimate feed costs, evaluate the average consumption per bison and the market price of feed. Veterinary services include routine health checks and emergency care. Keep a detailed log of these expenses to track fluctuations and adjust your budget as needed.

To create a comprehensive budget, consolidate all these costs and compare them with projected income from selling bison products such as meat, hides, or breeding stock. Use historical data from similar operations to make realistic income projections. Regularly review and adjust your budget to reflect any changes in costs or income. For instance, if feed prices increase, adjust your budget to accommodate these changes.

Financial Record-Keeping

Accurate financial record-keeping is essential for effective financial management in bison ranching. Start by setting up a system to track all financial transactions, including income and expenses. Use accounting software or a detailed ledger to record each transaction. Ensure that you categorize expenses accurately, such as feed, labor, veterinary care, and equipment maintenance.

Regularly update your records to reflect daily transactions and reconcile them with bank statements. This practice helps identify discrepancies and ensures accuracy. For instance, if you purchase a feed, record the amount spent and the vendor's details. At the end of each month, review your records to assess spending patterns and make adjustments as needed.

Maintain receipts, invoices, and other documentation to support your financial records. Store these documents in an organized manner, either physically or digitally. For tax purposes, it's essential to keep records for several years. Consider using cloud storage or an external hard drive to ensure the safety and accessibility of your financial records.

Investment And Funding Options

Investing in bison ranching can require significant capital, and understanding your funding options is crucial. Start by assessing your current financial situation and determining how much capital you need for initial setup and ongoing operations. Explore various funding options such as personal savings, bank loans, or grants.

Bank loans can be a viable option for funding large-scale investments. Prepare a detailed business plan outlining your budget, projected income, and repayment strategy to present to lenders. Interest rates and loan terms vary, so compare different offers to find the best fit for your needs.

Grants and subsidies from agricultural organizations or government programs can provide financial support. Research available programs and their eligibility requirements. Apply for grants by submitting detailed proposals and demonstrating how the funding will benefit your bison ranching operation. Additionally, consider partnerships or investors who might be interested in supporting your venture in exchange for a share of the profits.

Profitability Analysis

Conducting a profitability analysis helps assess the financial health of your bison ranching operation. Begin by calculating your gross profit margin, which is the difference between your total revenue and cost of goods sold. For instance, if you sell bison meat and earn $100,000 but incur $60,000 in costs, your gross profit is $40,000.

Next, analyze your net profit margin, which accounts for all expenses, including operating costs, interest, and taxes. Subtract these expenses from your gross profit to determine your net profit. For example, if your operating costs and taxes total $20,000, your net profit would be $20,000.

Regularly review your profitability by comparing current performance with previous periods and industry benchmarks. This analysis helps identify trends and areas for improvement. If your profit margins are declining, investigate potential causes such as rising costs or decreased sales, and adjust your strategies accordingly.

Risk Management Strategies

Effective risk management is crucial for minimizing potential setbacks in bison ranching. Start by identifying potential risks, such as disease outbreaks, market fluctuations, or extreme weather conditions.

Develop a risk management plan that includes preventive measures and contingency plans.

For disease prevention, implement a vaccination schedule and maintain proper sanitation practices. Regularly monitor your herd's health and establish protocols for addressing any signs of illness. To mitigate market risks, diversify your income sources by exploring additional revenue streams such as eco-tourism or bison-based products.

Prepare for weather-related risks by investing in weather-resistant infrastructure and maintaining an emergency fund. Ensure you have insurance coverage for your livestock, property, and equipment to protect against unexpected losses. Regularly review and update your risk management plan to address new challenges and changing circumstances.

CHAPTER TEN

Sustainability And Future Trends

Sustainable Bison Ranching Practices

Sustainable bison ranching is crucial for maintaining the health of the ecosystem while ensuring the viability of bison farming. A key component of sustainability is implementing rotational grazing systems. This involves dividing the pasture into smaller sections and rotating the bison through these sections periodically. By allowing pastures to rest and recover, you prevent overgrazing and promote healthy soil and plant growth. This method also helps to manage parasites and reduce the need for chemical interventions.

Another important practice is maintaining biodiversity within the grazing lands. By incorporating a variety of forage species, you enhance the nutritional quality of the diet for the bison and support a balanced ecosystem. Planting native grasses and legumes can improve soil health and reduce erosion. Additionally, maintaining wetlands and riparian zones on your ranch can provide essential habitat for wildlife and contribute to overall environmental health.

Water management is also a crucial aspect of sustainable bison ranching. Ensuring that your bison have access to clean, fresh water without overusing local water resources is vital. Implementing water conservation techniques such as rainwater harvesting and efficient irrigation systems can help minimize the environmental impact of your ranching activities.

Regularly checking and maintaining water troughs and fences will also prevent contamination and waste.

Environmental Impact Considerations

When considering the environmental impact of bison ranching, it's important to assess the effects of your practices on soil health, water quality, and local wildlife. Soil erosion can be a significant concern if pastures are overgrazed or if there is improper land management. To mitigate this, ensure that you follow best practices for grazing management, including proper stocking rates and rotational grazing.

Water quality can be affected by runoff from manure and fertilizers. Implementing buffer zones around water bodies and using riparian plantings can help filter runoff and protect aquatic ecosystems. Additionally, consider using manure management systems that compost waste efficiently, reducing potential contamination of water sources and minimizing greenhouse gas emissions.

Local wildlife can also be impacted by bison ranching practices. Providing wildlife corridors and maintaining natural habitats can help mitigate these effects. It's beneficial to monitor the impact of your ranching activities on local fauna and flora and make adjustments to your management practices as needed to protect biodiversity.

Innovations In Bison Farming

The bison farming industry is evolving with new technologies and practices designed to enhance efficiency and sustainability. One such innovation is the use of precision agriculture technologies. These technologies include GPS tracking and data analytics to monitor grazing patterns, pasture health, and bison movement. By using this data, ranchers can make informed decisions about pasture management and improve the overall health of their bison herd.

Another innovation is the development of advanced breeding techniques. Genetic testing and selective breeding can help improve the health and productivity of bison herds. By focusing on traits such as disease resistance and feed efficiency, ranchers can enhance the quality of their stock and reduce costs.

The integration of renewable energy sources is also gaining traction in bison farming. Solar panels and wind turbines can be used to power ranch operations, reducing reliance on fossil fuels and decreasing the carbon footprint of your ranch. Investing in renewable energy technologies can lead to long-term cost savings and contribute to a more sustainable farming operation.

Adapting To Market Changes

Adapting to market changes is essential for the success of any bison ranching operation. One way to stay ahead is by diversifying your product offerings. In addition to selling bison meat, consider value-added products such as bison jerky, leather goods, or processed meats. Diversification can help stabilize income and attract different customer segments.

Building strong relationships with buyers and exploring new markets can also be beneficial. Establishing connections with local restaurants, specialty food stores, and farmers' markets can create additional revenue streams. Additionally, staying informed about market trends and consumer preferences will allow you to adjust your product offerings and marketing strategies accordingly.

Marketing and branding are crucial for adapting to market changes. Developing a strong brand identity and promoting the unique qualities of your bison products can help differentiate your business in a competitive market. Utilizing social media and online platforms can increase visibility and reach a broader audience.

Planning For Long-Term Success

Planning for long-term success in bison ranching involves strategic planning and foresight. Start by setting clear, achievable goals for your ranching operation. These goals should include financial targets, herd management objectives, and sustainability milestones. Regularly reviewing and updating your business plan will help you stay on track and adapt to changing circumstances.

Investing in ongoing education and training for yourself and your team is also important. Staying current with industry advancements, best practices, and regulatory changes will help you maintain a competitive edge. Consider joining industry associations and attending conferences to network with other ranchers and gain valuable insights.

Financial planning and risk management are key components of long-term success. Develop a comprehensive budget that accounts for all expenses, including feed, veterinary care, and maintenance. Setting aside funds for unexpected costs and investing in insurance can help protect your business from unforeseen challenges. By being proactive and prepared, you can ensure the long-term viability and success of your bison ranching operation.

Frequently Asked Question And Answers

What is bison ranching?

Bison ranching involves raising American bison (bison bison) for their meat, hides, and other products. It typically includes managing bison herds, providing appropriate grazing conditions, and handling their health and breeding.

What are the benefits of raising bison over cattle?

Bison are more disease-resistant, require less medication, and are generally hardier than cattle. They can thrive on rougher terrain and lower-quality forage, making them a sustainable option for various environments.

How many bison should I start with?

Starting with a small herd, such as 10-20 bison, allows you to learn the basics of bison management and gradually expand as you gain experience.

What do bison eat?

Bison primarily graze on grasses, but they also eat shrubs and forbs. They are adapted to a wide range of forage types and can survive on lower-quality feed compared to cattle.

What type of fencing is best for bison?

High, strong fencing is crucial for bison, as they can be very powerful and jump or push through weak fences. Electric fences or sturdy woven wire fences at least 5-6 feet high are recommended.

How much space do bison need?

Bison require ample space to roam. A general guideline is about 1-2 acres per bison, but this can vary based on the quality of the forage and the type of grazing management.

What are the common health issues in bison?

Common health issues in bison include parasites, pneumonia, and foot problems. Regular health checks and proper management practices can help prevent and address these issues.

How do you handle bison?

Handling bison requires patience and care. They are more unpredictable than cattle, so using low-stress handling techniques and having secure facilities is essential. Professional assistance or training may be necessary for handling.

What is the best breeding strategy for bison?

Breeding strategies should focus on genetic diversity and health. Controlled mating and selection of bulls and cows based on health, size, and desirable traits help improve the herd's overall quality.

How much does it cost to start a bison ranch?

Initial costs include purchasing bison, fencing, shelter, equipment, and land. Costs can vary widely depending on location, scale, and specific needs, but starting a small operation can range from a few thousand to several tens of thousands of dollars.

How long does it take for bison to reach market weight?

Bison typically take 18-24 months to reach market weight, depending on their diet, genetics, and management practices.

Do bison require special care during winter?

Bison are well adapted to cold weather and can handle winter conditions if they have access to shelter and sufficient forage. However, monitoring their health and providing supplemental feed during harsh conditions is important.

Can bison be kept with other livestock?

Bison can be kept with other livestock, but it's essential to monitor interactions as bison can be more aggressive and dominant. Proper management and fencing are necessary to prevent conflicts.

What are the market opportunities for bison products?

Bison meat is considered a premium product due to its lean nature and unique flavor. Bison hides, bones, and other products also have niche markets, including specialty food stores and artisans.

How do you market bison meat?

Marketing bison meat involves creating a strong brand, reaching out to local markets, restaurants, and specialty stores, and educating consumers about the benefits of bison meat.

Are there any government programs or subsidies for bison ranching?

Some government programs and subsidies may be available for bison ranchers, including conservation programs, grants, and tax incentives. Check with local agricultural extension offices or government agencies for specific opportunities.

What are the main challenges in bison ranching?

Challenges include managing large, powerful animals, ensuring proper fencing, and dealing with health issues, and market fluctuations. Careful planning and management can help mitigate these challenges.

How do bison adapt to different climates?

Bison are adaptable to a range of climates, from cold winters to hot summers. They have thick fur for insulation in winter and can tolerate high temperatures if they have access to water and shade.

What are the legal requirements for bison ranching?

Legal requirements vary by region and may include permits for livestock, adherence to animal welfare regulations, and compliance with land use zoning laws. It's important to check local regulations before starting a bison ranch.

How do you prepare for bison calving?

Bison calving requires the preparation of calving pens, monitoring for signs of labor, and providing a clean, safe environment. Regular check-ups and having a plan for any potential complications are important for successful calving.

CONCLUSION

Bison ranching represents a dynamic and sustainable agricultural practice that bridges the gap between ecological preservation and profitable land use. As we conclude our exploration of this fascinating industry, it is evident that bison ranching offers numerous benefits that extend beyond the realm of traditional cattle farming.

Firstly, bison ranching plays a crucial role in preserving and restoring native grasslands. Unlike cattle, bison have evolved with these ecosystems, contributing to the health and diversity of the prairie environment. Their grazing patterns help maintain the balance of plant species, promote soil fertility, and support a variety of wildlife. By choosing bison over traditional livestock, ranchers are actively participating in the conservation of important natural habitats, which is a significant ecological advantage.

Moreover, bison are remarkably resilient and require less input compared to other livestock. Their ability to thrive on natural forage, coupled with their resistance to many diseases and parasites, means that bison ranching can be a more cost-effective option. This resilience translates into lower feed costs and reduced need for veterinary care, making it an attractive choice for those looking to maintain a sustainable and profitable operation.

From a market perspective, bison meat is gaining popularity due to its nutritional benefits and environmental advantages. It is lower in fat and cholesterol compared to beef and is perceived as a healthier alternative. Additionally, as consumer awareness of sustainable and ethical food production grows, the demand for bison products is likely to increase.

This presents a promising opportunity for ranchers to tap into niche markets and differentiate their products.

However, it is important to acknowledge the challenges associated with bison ranching. The initial investment in fencing, handling facilities, and herd management can be substantial. Additionally, bison require specialized care and knowledge, which may necessitate further education and training for new ranchers. Despite these challenges, the long-term benefits and rewards of bison ranching can be substantial.

In conclusion, bison ranching represents a forward-thinking approach to livestock management that aligns with ecological stewardship and market trends. By integrating bison into their operations, ranchers can contribute to environmental conservation while benefiting from a sustainable and profitable agricultural enterprise.

As the industry continues to evolve, it holds promise for further innovations and growth, reinforcing the importance of bison ranching in modern agriculture.

THE END

www.ingramcontent.com/pod-product-compliance
Lightning Source LLC
Chambersburg PA
CBHW071834210526
45479CB00001B/133